Your Amazing Itty Bitty™ Grief Journey 101

15 Key Steps to Heal and Live Again

Dr. Kimberly Q. Hubenette

Published by Itty Bitty™ Publishing
A subsidiary of S & P Productions, Inc.

Your Amazing Itty Bitty Grief Journey 101

Printed in the United States of America

Itty Bitty Publishing
311 Main Street, Suite D
El Segundo, CA 90245
(310) 640-8885

ISBN: 978-1-959964-71-1

This book is for educational purposes only. Nothing should be taken as mental health advice, diagnosis or treatment. Always seek the guidance of a mental health professional should you need assistance.

Dedication

This book is dedicated to the love I lost: my Mark and the life I found on the other side.

To every broken heart that still beats, and to every soul that chooses to get up every morning.

To everyone who whispers, " I will live again," this book is for you.

For your courage, your tears, and the strength you may not yet see.

You are not alone.

Your healing matters.

And your journey is sacred.

To my family, friends, and staff members who have always stood by my side in all the impulsive, impractical projects I place myself into, and to those who march to their own tune, I believe in you. You are my inspiration.

Stop by our Itty Bitty™ website to find interesting information regarding Grief Journey 101:15 Key Steps to Heal and Live Again

www.IttyBittyPublishing.com

Or visit Kimberly Q. Hubenette, DDS, MAGD, LLSR at

www.drkimberlyhubenette.com

Table of Contents

Introduction

And just like that, your life changed! What now? In these pages I have outlined the five stages of grief the way I recognized them when I went through my grief journey. This definition is easy to understand. It will guide you through your healing journey from emergency mode to thrive mode. Each stage brings its own challenges, and you may spend more time in one than another.

1. Emergency mode: You're emotionally overwhelmed and mentally stuck in a survival state that can lead to self-destruction if prolonged.
2. Remedial mode: Life becomes mechanical. You're just getting by, handling only what is urgent.
3. Self-help mode: You begin to reengage, helping others and offering hope, even if your solutions are still short-term.
4. Complete mode: You're committed to true healing. With long-term goals and purpose, you begin to build a meaningful life again, carrying your loved one with you in memory.
5. Thrive mode: You embrace life fully, living not just for yourself but with the joy your loved one would have

wanted for you. You are open to love, adventure, and new beginnings.

The traditional five stages of grief, as defined by Elisabeth Kubler-Ross, are emotional responses to loss. They serve as one model of understanding grief. My own interpretation is rooted in innate coping mechanisms rather than emotional stages.

There are lasting consequences to every decision you make, especially in times of loss. Your choices today influence the trajectory of your future. Whether you choose to seek new opportunities or remain anchored in the past, healing is not linear. It can take years, or even a lifetime. Only you will know when it is time to ask for help. This book is here as a guide to support you through each stage of your grief journey.

With Love!
Dr. Kimberly Q. Hubenette

Step 1
Devastation

Whether you have lost your spouse, child, or another loved one, the grief cycle has many stages. You may be in shock or in denial. You may not want to get out of bed, you may be feeling numb inside, and you may not know what you're doing. If you're walking around like a zombie, you're not alone. This is normal. If you feel you want to eliminate everything and everyone from your life, this is normal.

1. You may feel devastation.
2. You may feel shocked.
3. You may feel numb, like nothing else will ever matter again.

Losing someone shatters your world as you knew it. It can feel like time stands still. The depth of sorrow is not only emotional; it is physical, spiritual, and all-encompassing. Devastation is a natural response to love, and a reflection of how deeply you cared. Pain will never fully disappear. However, you will learn to carry it with grace, finding light with no judgment and no regrets. Give your body permission to feel, heal, and live again.

More About Devastation

Overwhelm gets in the way; you may be unable to function for a while. You may also find that you cannot get out of bed except to let the dog out. Give yourself permission to heal. Life will go on, but you have to take the steps.

- Find a purpose to move forward.
- Remember, your living loved ones still need you.
- Take time off, but give yourself a time-line.
- Find your own way through.
- Do what you feel is right.

Whatever you do, your way is going to be your right way. You may need to write a letter to your loved one, or you may need to get closure by going to their favorite places. You may go with people or try to do it alone. However, you must still be able to function in life.

- Show up at work.
- Be there for your children.
- Be present for your pet.
- Be there for your staff members.
- Be there for your family.
- Be there for yourself.

Step 2
You Are Not Alone

You may feel that you are on a desert island with no inhabitants but yourself. But you're not alone. Understand that in your grief journey, there are two things that every human has in common: you are born, and you die. In the middle is your unique journey in life. Rest assured that you will find others who can relate to you. Opening your mind to change is just a twist in your path.

1. Share with your friends how you're feeling. You may be surprised that one or two will relate to what you're presently experiencing.
2. Join a social media group that vets their membership status for those with common interests.
3. Sit with a friend in silence. Energy will move through the room between each of you. Silence between two people is still being together.
4. Find a local support group that you can connect with.
5. Volunteer at a charity of your interest.

More About You Are Not Alone

Life experiences can create bonds with people you never related to in the past. Feel and connect with yourself to build a better relationship with *you.* You may find you can grieve in comfort. Be it with a grief support group or a new hobby group, taking action is the only way to change how you're feeling.

- Brainstorm a list of friends who have had a loved one pass.
- Scroll through your social media to find interesting groups that appeal to you.
- List some hobbies that you may be interested in.

Put yourself out there and take action. Curveballs in life can be the one thing that helps you get to the next level in your grief journey.

- Participate and show up.
- Ask for support from your friends and family.
- Create memories with new people.
- Take a class in your community.
- Make play dates with your dog's friends.
- Make play dates with your children's friends.
- Make play dates with your friends.

Step 3
Finding Signs From Above

Finding signs from above refers to after-death communication, and it's comforting if you let yourself be vulnerable to them. Signs can manifest in many forms. The message could be guidance from a spiritual leader or a fortune teller. It could be in a dream, or encountering certain objects or symbols. It could be seeing a certain animal. These meaningful messages can be received as comforting messages from your loved one if you believe in this.

1. Finding coins such as pennies, nickels, or dimes may be of personal significance.
2. Seeing a favorite animal, such as a butterfly, a flock of ducks, or doves, may be peaceful to you.
3. Seeing the same number everywhere you turn may be a sign that he/she is with you.
4. The same flickering light may be the message you need when you speak to your loved one.

You may wonder about the meaning of the message that came to you. It could be validation that the path you're about to embark on is the right path for you. It could be a way you speak to your loved one, and they answer back.

More About Signs From Above

Although you may not always understand the message, there are signs surrounding you from above. Be open to these signs and look for them.

- Listen for a favorite song to come on the radio.
- Look for flickering lights.
- Find that rainbow in the sky after rain.
- Take comfort in finding a sign that only your loved one would have known about.
- Signs from above can be comforting, encouraging, and validating.
- Signs from above may appear when you least expect them.

Signs can be interpreted as love, support, and encouragement. Whatever it may be for you, these signs from above can help you feel better about your decision to move forward on your path to healing in your grief journey.

- What is the meaning of this message?
- Is it the answer you have been waiting for from your loved one?
- Is it the justification you need to make your next decision?
- Is it confirmation that you made the right move?

Step 4
Lists! Lists! Lists!

The next step is gathering information after you realize your loved one will truly never walk through your front door again. There are several tasks and arrangements that must be done, like it or not. Creating a binder or a digital document to establish one location for all your to-do tasks is important to keep yourself going. You may choose to buy a bound book of lists compiled by a trusted source. Sometimes the simplest of tasks can be missed. Here are some suggestions to start your lists.

1. Separate your journal/digital documents and categorize the lists immediately as short-term, long-term, and other tasks.
2. Timeline each section as it pertains to priority: weeks, months, or even years. Not all tasks are of the same value.
3. Contact your estate attorney, CPA, and trusted friends to help you.
4. Delegate people who can help you start or complete your tasks.
5. Take bite-sized pieces.
6. Lists are organizational tasks that can help you for a lifetime if mastered.

More About Lists! Lists! Lists!

After sectioning off your document, become granular and specific. The most common must-dos for immediate arrangements are as follows:

- Obtain a legal certificate of death and a medical certification, and make 10 copies.
- Delegate who will list and notify each friend and family member for you.
- Locate documents that might have details of your loved one's last wishes, estate documents, will/trust, insurance policies, bank deposit box, etc.
- Organ donation: Immediately notify the coroner and medical team.
- Write the obituary or give the task to someone who can do an exceptional job. Proof it for accuracy.

Reminder that you must keep funding the bank accounts that pay your loved one's bills. Do not let your insurance premiums or utility bills lapse.

- Keep paying all bills, loans, and taxes.
- Lock the bank accounts and credit cards as soon as possible. Predators can sabotage and ruin your loved one's identity and credit rating within days of death.
- Look for passwords to secure all accounts. Do not forget social media pages.
- If you are past the emergency stage, mastering lists will help you organize the long-term tasks of your grief journey.

Step 5
Write a Letter

If you have unanswered questions that represent a lack of information and you're unable to move past them, it may be therapeutic to write a letter to your deceased loved one. This tool helps to process your grief and may help you break through to help you reach the next stage in your journey.

1. A letter may not necessarily mean that you're in denial; it's a form of inner communication.
2. A letter may help you express emotions that you were unable to present in person.
3. A letter can be written to discuss unfinished business, provide closure, and help with forgiveness or apologies.
4. Write a letter with your dominant hand and use your non-dominant hand as the way that your loved one answers you back. You may be surprised what happens next.

More About Writing a Letter

There are multiple ways to write to your loved one. This type of communication may help you keep the connection ongoing. In this modern age, there are several ways to write to your deceased loved one.

- Handwrite a letter to your loved one.
- Text a message to their phone number.
- Send an email to your loved one.
- Create a private post to your loved one's social media page.

Writing to your loved one is very therapeutic and happens more often than you think. You can consider this a method to continue throughout your lifetime should you choose.

- Find closure to a particular situation.
- Find peace that you made the right decision.
- Find reassurance that you chose the right path.
- Find joy in sharing happy moments of life through ongoing communication.
- Allow yourself to write.
- Don't let others discourage you from writing to your deceased loved one.
- If it makes you happy, write regularly.
- If you're unable to write, speak it out loud.

Step 6
Daily Rituals

Daily routines are helpful to keep you on track to get through your day when you feel it's hard to move forward. Morning rituals can nurture your mind to start believing in life again. Here are a few examples that you can try.

1. Take time for yourself. Wake up and stretch in bed.
2. Take time to acknowledge and love yourself with positive daily affirmations.
3. Deep breathing exercises give needed oxygen to the brain, where neurons regrow as we breathe.
4. Creating a reflection book and journaling your daily goals may keep you on track to get things done.

Find simple, low-effort rituals that work for you to make it easier to get through your day with less stress and more ease. State your name, then speak to yourself in the mirror with an affirmation.

1. "Name, you are amazing, you are joyful, you are loved, you are here."
2. "Name, you breathe in peace and exhale stress."
3. "Name, each moment is a chance to begin again."

More About Daily Rituals

Each moment with yourself is a chance to begin again. When you perform your breathing exercises, breathe in peace, hold for 10 seconds, and exhale stress. As you do your exercises, think about the following things.

- Choose to trust the process and believe in your path to move forward.
- Choose to speak kindly to yourself each day.
- Choose to honor your needs without guilt or apology.

As you perform your daily rituals, whether it be morning or evening, know that progress is not perfection. Tackle one thing at a time, and know it's okay for you to move at your own pace. Even little wins count.

- Take time to give yourself grace and rest along the way.
- Journal your goals, including your ups and downs.
- One day, you will read your book of reflections, and know that you have overcome your anxiety and conquered your grief.

Step 7
Moving Through Your Grief

Grief has many levels. Your grief is unique to you. You can experience many different feelings: joy, sorrow, anger, and pain can arise at any stage. There is no set path or timeline.

1. It's okay to laugh out loud and then cry.
2. It's okay to cry, then laugh out loud.
3. You can be at any level of grief and have the same emotions emerge again and again.

You may move quickly through one mode and linger in another. What matters is taking small daily steps. Even if you never reach thrive, every stage has emotions and is part of healing. That's enough for your happiness and success.

1. Moving through the stages depends upon your level of mental focus and emotional soundness.
2. It's what you do with what you learn about yourself that determines where you will end up in your journey.
3. You will have emotional outbursts in all stages of grief. Harness your emotions; use them to help keep you happy and successful, to thrive in life.

More About Moving Through Your Grief

Know your strengths and weaknesses as you move through your grief journey.

- List the most common recurring emotions that trigger you.
- Create daily rituals that calm you down.
- Understand what triggers your weaknesses.
- Journaling goals will help you get to the next level.
- Network with people who can help you.

Utilize your strengths to guide and create your healing path.

- List your aspirations in work and personal life.
- List activities that interest you.
- Create a vision board to remind you of your goals.
- Life is full of opportunities to thrive.
- Make a list of 50 things you want to do or travel to (your bucket list).
- Remember that your loved one would want you to thrive.

Step 8
Celebrating Traditions

Across cultures, honoring the dead takes many forms: some quiet, some festive, all rooted in meaningful traditions. These practices remind you that grief, commemoration, and celebration often walk hand in hand. An annual remembrance creates space for your ongoing reflection and connection.

1. Chinese cultures set out favorite food dishes on a loved one's birthday.
2. Mexican culture celebrates the Day of the Dead by creating a shrine with candles, food, and photos to welcome and honor the spirits.
3. Japan's Obon festival features lanterns and dances to guide ancestral spirits home and back again.
4. In New Orleans, jazz funerals include mourning and celebration-of-life music through a soulful procession.
5. Christians celebrate November 2 to honor and pray for the dead.
6. China celebrates in early April to clean tombstones, offer favorite foods, and pay respects.
7. Nepal honors those who died that year with a colorful parade and celebration.

More About Celebrating Traditions

Even if you don't have a familial cultural tradition, you can start one of your own. Start an annual tradition to memorialize your loved one.

- Create a playlist to listen to your favorite songs.
- Plan an annual trip to a favorite vacation spot.
- Do a favorite activity you enjoyed together: camp, fish, hike, draw, paint.
- Drive your loved one's car around on their birthday and blast their favorite song.
- Eat at your loved one's special restaurant.
- Set out a favorite meal and eat it in front of their picture to let them watch you.
- Watch your loved one's favorite movie.

Plan an annual single event or a multiple-day excursion of events. Plan a trip to a place you both had on your wish lists that never happened. There's no right or wrong. It's whatever makes you happy and connected to your loved one that matters.

- Plan a trip to a location you were planning to visit but never went to together.
- Plan a hike or pilgrimage to a destination location from their wish list. (Example: Camino de Santiago, Half Dome, Pacific Crest Trail, or just a favorite local spot).

Step 9
Get Out of Bed; Stop Being a ZOMBIE!

You're completely normal when you feel overwhelmed. When you wake up, you may not want to get out of bed. Whether you couldn't sleep the night before or you don't want to face the day, life continues to move around you.

1. You will experience difficulty with everyday tasks.
2. It's a natural part of the grieving process.
3. You will go through a zombie phase; just don't stay there.
4. It takes time to heal.

Although you may feel like a zombie, you have to get through this stage. When you wake up, give yourself credit for even deciding to get out of bed. Slowly add tasks to your routine one day at a time.

1. Acknowledge your emotions and feelings for the day.
2. Embrace your day with a new outlook on life.
3. Make a plan with a friend or co-worker to achieve one task each day.
4. Go outside, look up at the sky, and say hello to the world.

More About Get Out of Bed; Stop Being a ZOMBIE!

Prioritize what you do before you go to bed so you get enough rest. Sometimes feeling like a zombie results from actions or nonactions you took the night before.

- Reflect on the prior day to understand how you can feel better the next day.
- Did you move enough to work off energy?
- Did you eat too late?
- Did you drink too much caffeine the night before?
- Did you allow enough time to sleep?
- Did you intentionally stay up too late?

Take time to consider your daily schedule to help you get out of bed in the morning. It will have a direct impact on the quality of your day.

- Think about what your loved one would do if they were you.
- Think about how you would live their day.
- What actions will you take to be productive tomorrow?
- Replace negative habits with positive beginnings.

Step 10
Give It Away (Keep Special Items)

Giving away belongings is deeply personal and challenging. The process of letting go may take months or years to finish. Do not get rid of things out of pain and suffering. The challenge is having enough time to process without regret before you give it away. You must let go to make room for new beginnings, but keep special items.

1. Will you use this item yourself?
2. If not, will it be better off with a friend or family member?
3. Can a family member or best friend use this item lovingly?
4. Do you have multiples of this item? Can someone else utilize it?

Sentimental value comes from within ourselves. You must define in your mind if the item is worth being stored or whether it could be used by someone new. Don't be selfish about your items.

1. Would a friend or family member cherish an item from your deceased loved one?
2. Can the item impact the lives of others?
3. Will it just sit in your closet, or will you use it?

More About Give It Away (Keep Special Items)

Cherish the moments you had with the item, take a picture of it before you give it away or sell it. Remember that old energy could be keeping you from exploring a newer you.

- Was this item really what you thought it meant to your loved one?
- Did you place the right meaning on this item?
- Acknowledge and thank the item for being in your life before you give it away.

You can do this. Approach this task with sensitivity and make time to do it lovingly.

- Ask your loved one's friends to help you look over items you know little about.
- Give a special item to your loved one's best friend.
- Give a special item to your loved one's mom, dad, or sibling.
- Give a special item to your loved one's child.
- There are opportunities to touch the lives of your loved one's inner circle if you just take the time to think about it.
- You will feel good about giving the item away.

Step 11
Your Health and Wellness

Whether you let yourself go or you've always been health-conscious has everything to do with self-awareness during your grief journey. You may think you were doing a good job at looking and being healthy, but have you looked in the mirror lately?

1. Be aware of what you look like to others.
2. Is your nutritional intake sufficient for healthy living?
3. Are you exercising or moving around with intention?
4. Are you drinking at least 36 ounces of water daily?
5. The basic maintenance of cleanliness, such as taking a shower, brushing your teeth, and brushing your hair can be overlooked.

You may need an occasional reminder to keep yourself tidy when you're grieving. This is normal.

1. Ask a trusted friend if you're looking healthy.
2. When you ask, you must be open to the truth (constructive criticism).
3. Replace your negative habits with positive, consistent behaviors.

More About Your Health and Wellness

Daily tasks that get overlooked with time can be detrimental in the long run. Encourage yourself to improve and do a fresh restart for your well-being. Experiment with a new side of yourself. Test a version of yourself you haven't explored yet. You may be surprised that you feel more energized.

- Your body creates endorphins during movement that give you more energy to make healthier choices.
- To become more alive, you must actively choose positive change.
- Limit your exposure to fast foods and choose salads and fruits.
- Walk up a flight of stairs instead of taking the elevator.
- Ride your bike instead of driving.

Following these simple changes can be self-preserving and help you achieve better health.

- Stay committed to changes, and you will feel the difference.
- Transformations take time and commitment.
- Focus on health and wellness.
- Commit to yourself, and you will soon see the difference in your life.
- Seek help from a professional or your faith community to guide you through this healing process.

Step 12
Stay Away From Negative People

Negativity can come from people as well as situations. Recognizing and removing yourself from negative influences will help you transform and cultivate new habits. Your friends and family might unintentionally downplay the significance of your loss, or even show toxic positivity toward you.

1. Do not let people invalidate your emotions. You must be able to express yourself.
2. Stay away from people who overemphasize not crying or talking about your loved one.
3. Do not let others compare or judge the way you're grieving.
4. Be aware that grieving drains energy; be mindful of the amount of time you give yourself daily to grieve.

Adopt the 80/20 rule by grieving 80% and being productive 20%, and gradually lower the percentage of time you stay in grieving mode.

1. This is easier said than done; give yourself a goal to follow to support change.
2. Cultivate new relationships and new activeities with the 80/20 rule.

More About Stay Away From Negative People

Ask your friends and family for what you need. They may need your guidance to know how to act around you. Don't be surprised if your friends disappear for a while, and don't be surprised if they're overly nurturing.

- Set boundaries with your family and friends.
- Don't let them project their emotions onto you.
- Identify your needs and what drains your energy.
- Consider the topics that are off limits to you.
- It's okay to say no to invitations from friends, family, and coworkers.

If your friends repeatedly cross your off-limit zone, it's okay to disengage from them for a while. Pause before responding to avoid negative confrontations.

- Politely state, "I appreciate your concern; however, it's not helping me."
- "I appreciate you thinking about me, but I'm not ready to discuss __________."
- Remember that your situation is unique to you. Only you know how best to help yourself.
- Seek the advice of a professional who supports your needs.

Step 13
Find Your Purpose

You're in transition, and you've lost your sense of purpose. Don't isolate yourself from the world; get out and do something. Grief runs its course, yet you're ready to seek a new life path. If you do not find your purpose, you'll stay in an abyss forever. Your purpose could be short- or long-term, or small or large projects. Encourage yourself with these simple steps to move forward.

1. Check out local events in your area, such as nonprofits or activity groups.
2. Create a list of ideas that may be interesting to pursue.
3. List projects you need to start, follow up on, or finish.
4. Does a dependent child or pet need your attention?
5. What areas are being neglected—health, business, bills, home, or dependents?

After you've created your lists, it's time to narrow your choices.

1. Circle at least three items that resonate with you.
2. Use highlighters for first-to-third priority options for each category of interest.

More About Find Your Purpose

Now that you've narrowed the ideas with priority lists, rewrite each highlighted idea as separate headings in your journal.

- What do you hope to achieve with each idea/project?
- What will you need to do to start? What can you start today?
- Who will do it with you?
- Does it involve money, time, or budget?
- Is your purpose a business, hobby, or pet?

Get granular with each priority idea on your list. Don't get bogged down in perfection before you start your idea. Become the person you want to be. Do the thing you choose to become, and you'll have the outcome you desire. If you don't act, you'll never move forward. Focus on your long- and short-term ideas, as follows.

- Initiate the *be, do, have* concepts.
- Call, email, or text an event coordinator.
- Learn about Rotary, Kiwanis, and church leadership.
- Adopt a pet.
- Foster a child, dog, or cat.
- Start home repairs.
- Reorganize your house.
- Reorganize a new or old business.
- Network with a coach, group, or special interest group.

Step 14
Get Out There (Check Off Your Bucket List)

You're transforming into a bolder you to stretch your inner being to remind yourself that you're alive. Create and conquer your bucket list: vacations, career challenges, or hobbies. You're ready to do this.

1. Challenge yourself to one bold goal that stretches you to feel alive.
2. Book a destination vacation you've never been to before.
3. Create your perfect workday and do it for one day, one week, one month.
4. Book a class for a hobby you've always envisioned for yourself.

Once you visualize these goals, you can see them as attainable. A new, renewed lifestyle awaits you as you conquer your fears of living to the fullest.

1. Take a leap of faith, knowing you can achieve it.
2. Challenge yourself and write it on your bathroom mirror.
3. Seeing is believing; create a vision board and view it daily until it's achieved.
4. Use a virtual reality simulator to see simulations of your possible future.

More About Get Out There (Check Off Your Bucket List)

When you've reached a point in your grief journey, and you're ready to tackle harder goals, you will be ready to add harder tasks.

- Envision adding layers to your life that you never dreamed you could accomplish.
- Set your standards higher to stretch yourself.
- Help a friend or find an accountability partner to create your bucket list.

You're ready to dream big. Your bucket list of goals may take days, weeks, or years to achieve.

- Buy a bucket list book of ideas.
- Start a group if you can't find one that fits your goals.
- Join an online group that fits your goals.
- Read magazines for ideas to add to your bucket list of dreams.
- Create a vision board with pictures of your bucket list.
- Invent something or a process that's never been done before.

Step 15
Live, Love, Survive, Thrive

The last step has four parts and is the most challenging. Each day, moment, and task you do on this earth is meaningful in your life. Although your loved one is deceased, you can still include them in your life journey. Surround yourself with their memory and choose to live the fullest life at the same time.

1. Living your fullest life will be your task to determine.
2. Loving your environment or finding a new love doesn't mean your loved one is forgotten. Be thankful for the time you had with them.
3. Create moments that reflect your new journey and memories.

Struggling to survive and thrive in your life are two distinct interpretations. Choose the latter, and you will flourish. Take the best version of yourself and move forward to create an extraordinary lifestyle.

1. Be eager to live again. Living is what you are supposed to do on this earth.
2. Choose to love who you are, what you do, and who you do it with.
3. Your loved one would have wanted you to keep living and loving to the fullest.

More About Live, Love, Survive, Thrive

Challenge yourself to survive and thrive at the same time. Change can be simple or extreme, as long as you're true to yourself. You will find your way. Don't regret or wallow in doubt. Your mind is a powerful tool to help you continue living.

- Challenge yourself to survive by becoming your family's legacy.
- Help a friend get through their first steps of grief. Teaching ensures that you help yourself.
- You have unwritten life chapters to tackle, or they won't be discovered for future generations.

You can achieve anything you set your mind to. Be proactive in your next life chapters and be the embodiment of your choice.

- Become your children's legacy.
- Create new innovations never envisioned until now.
- Continue daily learning to keep a constant never-ending improvement mindset.
- Believe in yourself to overcome your challenges.
- Thrive in life by taking action!

You've finished. Before you go …

Post/share that you finished this book.

Please star rate this book.

Reviews are solid gold to writers. Please take a few minutes to give us some itty bitty feedback.

ABOUT THE AUTHOR

Dr. Kimberly Q. Hubenette is a Chinese-American dentist who has devoted over 30+ years to helping people smile with confidence and live with greater well-being. Her work is more than clinical skill. It reflects empathy, artistry, and a belief that healing the mouth can be part of healing the whole person. Through integrative, compassionate care, she has witnessed how restoring a smile can also restore spirit, self-worth, and hope.

When Dr. Kimberly's husband, Mark, passed away, grief became her unexpected teacher. Mark, a survivor of cystic fibrosis, lived 21 years more after receiving a double lung transplant; years he never took for granted. He poured his strength into an outdoor lifestyle, quiet wilderness rituals, and volunteer service with Sonoma Search and Rescue. His extraordinary resilience and his gift of breath through an organ transplant later inspired Dr. Kimberly's fiction novel, GRID, with its themes of survival, courage, and starting over.

In the aftermath of loss, she learned that grief reshapes us, revealing its pain as proof of great love. Through spiritual seeking, reflective writing, deep inner work, and allowing her life to move at its own rhythm, she discovered that grief can transform rather than destroy. These lessons inspired her to write *Your Amazing Itty Bitty™ Grief Journey 101:15 Key Steps to Heal and Live Again*, offering others the compassion, simplicity, and encouragement she once needed herself. In her writing and teachings, Dr. Kimberly reminds grieving hearts that love does not end; it changes form. It becomes memory, ritual, connection, and strength. Her work encourages readers to breathe again, seek new meaning, and allow a renewed self to emerge, one who carries ache, beauty, and the ability to choose to continue to grow.

Outside her professional world, Dr. Kimberly finds grounding and peace outdoors by hiking, walking her dog, Dakota, and spending quiet time in nature. These moments keep her connected to Mark's spirit, his love for wild places, and the healing found in open skies and stillness.

Today, she continues her mission through dentistry, storytelling, community connection, and her podcast *Live, Love, Survive, Thrive!,* and walking beside others through grief and reminding them that there is no perfect path: only the brave decision to keep living, loving, surviving, and eventually thriving.

If you enjoyed this Itty Bitty™ book, you might also like…

- **Your Amazing Itty Bitty™ Grief Book** – Lisa Y. Harrington
- **Your Amazing Itty Bitty™ Grief to Grace Book** – Dr. Sherry Shoemaker
- **Your Amazing Itty Bitty™ Getting Financially Organized Trilogy** – Marie Burns

Or any of the many Amazing Itty Bitty™ books available online at www.ittybittypublishing.com